WHSmith

Revise

Maths

KS1: YEAR 2
Book 2

Age 6–7

Paul Broadbent and
Peter Patilla

The *WHS Revise* series

The *WHS Revise* books enable you to help your child revise and practise important skills taught in school. These skills form part of the National Curriculum and will help your child to improve his or her Maths and English.

Testing in schools

During their time at school all children will undergo a variety of tests. Regular testing is a feature of all schools. It is carried out:

- *informally* – in everyday classroom activities your child's teacher is continually assessing and observing your child's performance in a general way
- *formally* – more regular formal testing helps the teacher check your child's progress in specific areas.

Testing is important because:

- it provides evidence of your child's achievement and progress
- it helps the teacher decide which skills to focus on with your child
- it helps compare how different children are progressing.

The importance of revision

Regular revision is important to ensure your child remembers and practises skills he or she has been taught. These books will help your child revise and test his or her knowledge of some of the things he or she will be expected to know. They will help you prepare your child to be in a better position to face tests in school with confidence.

How to use this book

Units

This book is divided into twenty units, each focusing on one key skill. Each unit begins with a **Remember** section, which introduces and revises essential information about the particular skill covered. If possible, read and discuss this with your child to ensure he or she understands it.

This is followed by a **Have a go** section, which contains a number of activities to help your child revise the topic thoroughly and use the skill effectively. Usually, your child should be able to undertake these activities fairly independently.

Revision tests

There are two revision tests in this book (pages 24–27). These test the skills covered in the preceding units and assess your child's progress and understanding. They can be marked by you or by your child. Your child should fill in his or her test score for each test in the space provided. This will provide a visual record of your child's progress and an instant sense of confidence and achievement.

Parents' notes

The parents' notes (on pages 28–29) provide you with brief information on each skill and explain why it is important.

Answers

Answers to the unit questions and tests may be found on pages 30–32.

First published 2007
exclusively for WHSmith by
Hodder Education, part of Hachette Livre UK,
338 Euston Road
London
NW1 3BH

Impression number   10 9 8 7 6 5 4 3 2
Year   2008

Text and illustrations © Hodder Education 2007

A CIP record for this book is available from the British Library.

Cover illustration by Sally Newton Illustrations

Typeset by Fakenham Photosetting Limited, Fakenham, Norfolk

ISBN 978 034 0942 666

Printed and bound in Italy.

Contents

Remember

Numbers 10 to 99 have two **digits**.

This shows the tens
50

58
fifty-eight

This shows the ones
8

Use these to help you read and write numbers to 100.

20 twenty   40 forty   60 sixty   80 eighty

30 thirty   50 fifty   70 seventy   90 ninety

Have a go

1 Write the missing numbers or words.

a [ ] thirty-four   b 67 [ ]

c [ ] fifty-nine   d 28 [ ]

e [ ] seventy-two   f 93 [ ]

g [ ] sixty-six   h 45 [ ]

2 Complete this number puzzle.

Across
a thirty-four
b twenty-six
e sixty-one
f thirty-five

Down
a thirty-seven
c sixty-three
d fifty-two
e sixty-eight
g fifty-nine

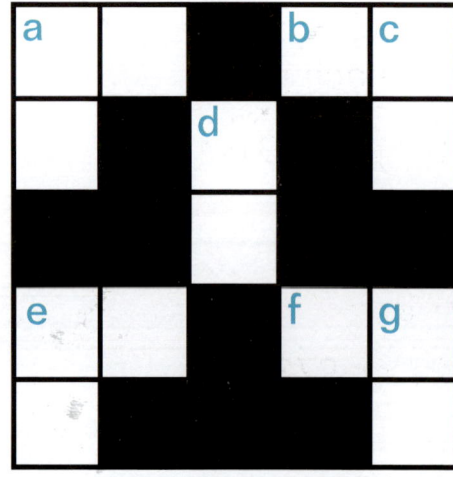

Unit 2: Comparing numbers

Remember

When you compare **two-digit numbers** to see which is bigger or smaller, look at the **tens** and then the **ones** digit.

45 is larger than 38 because 4 tens is more than 3 tens.

Use this number line to help.

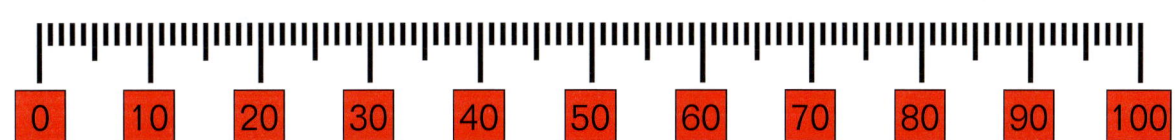

| 0 | 10 | 20 | 30 | 40 | 50 | 60 | 70 | 80 | 90 | 100 |

Have a go

1 Write the numbers that come between each of these star numbers.

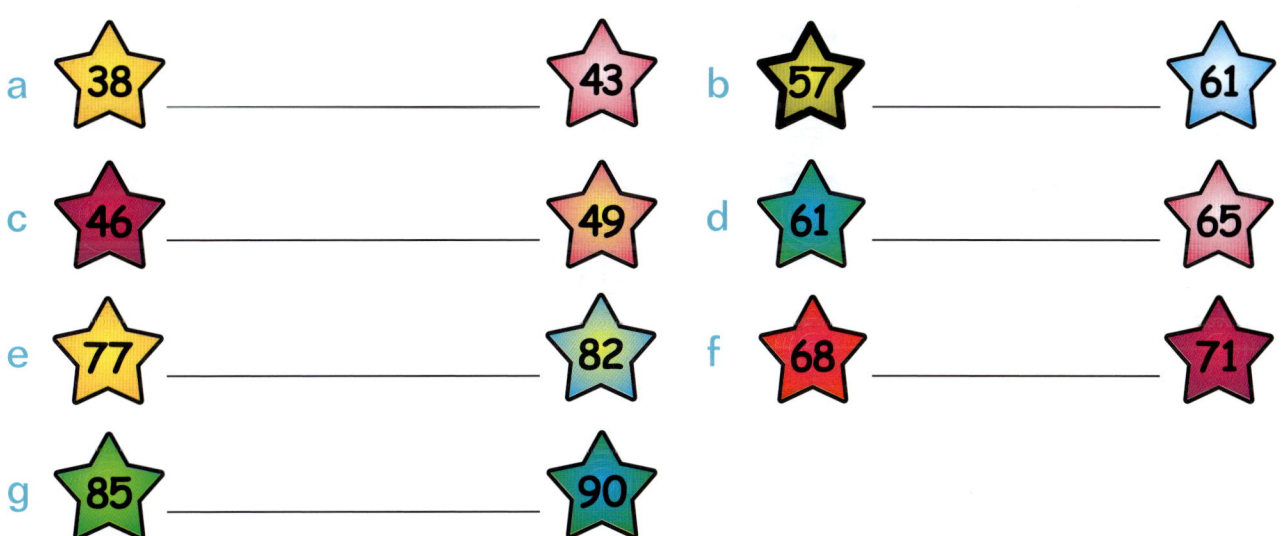

a 38 _____ 43   b 57 _____ 61

c 46 _____ 49   d 61 _____ 65

e 77 _____ 82   f 68 _____ 71

g 85 _____ 90

2 Circle the larger amount in each pair.

a 76 m or 67 m   b 48 cm or 39 cm

c 59 kg or 72 kg   d 96p or 78p

e £46 or £53   f 81 g or 97 g

g 63p or 67p   h £37 or £73

i 67 kg or 49 kg   j 10 cm or 18 cm

Remember

Use a **number line** to help with counting on and back.

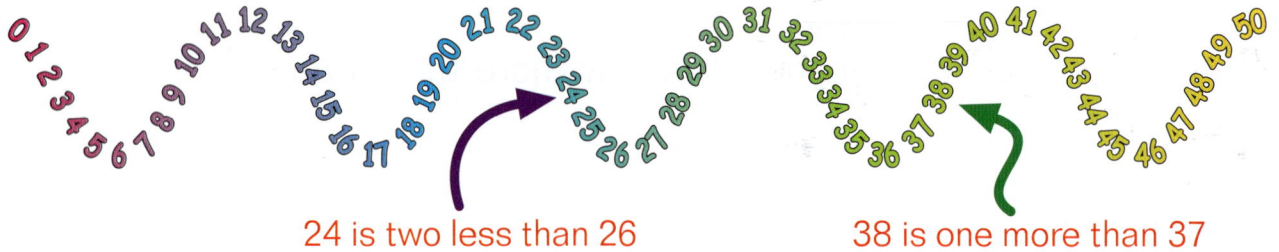

24 is two less than 26   38 is one more than 37

Have a go

1 Answer these. Use the number line to help you.

a one more than 28 ➡ ☐

b three more than 37 ➡ ☐

c one less than 45 ➡ ☐

d four more than 29 ➡ ☐

e two less than 41 ➡ ☐

f three less than 36 ➡ ☐

g two more than 46 ➡ ☐

h four less than 43 ➡ ☐

2 Write the missing numbers in each sequence.

a | 46 | ☐ | 48 | 49 | 50 | ☐ | 52 |

b | 63 | 64 | ☐ | 66 | ☐ | 68 | 69 |

c | 72 | ☐ | 70 | 69 | 68 | 67 |

d | 85 | 84 | ☐ | ☐ | 81 | 80 | 79 |

Remember

Even numbers always end in 2, 4, 6, 8 or 0.

Odd numbers always end in 1, 3, 5, 7 or 9.

So 54 is an even number and 45 is an odd number.

Have a go

1 Write the missing numbers in each sequence

a 11 13 __ 17 __ 21

b 16 18 20 __ __ 26

c __ 27 __ 23 21 19

d 34 36 __ 40 __ 44

e 34 __ 30 28 26 __

f 49 __ __ 43 41 39

2 Colour the odd numbers red. Colour the even numbers blue.

What number have you made? _____

52	38	22	16	28	4	52	68	6	84	92	36	28	40	22	80
21	45	63	9	15	34	55	17	23	45	26	5	18	16	12	65
40	24	81	18	16	70	83	94	62	34	14	17	21	14	4	49
64	32	53	14	48	66	65	3	19	23	38	25	14	83	50	45
38	50	25	26	56	74	27	84	58	18	12	47	22	78	79	57
26	12	11	34	92	38	31	93	57	19	6	59	34	30	92	63

Unit 5: Fractions – quarters

Remember

When you cut a cake into four equal pieces, each piece is one quarter of the whole cake.

To find $\frac{1}{4}$ (one quarter) of these eight nuts, put them into four equal groups.

$\frac{1}{4}$ of 8 = 2

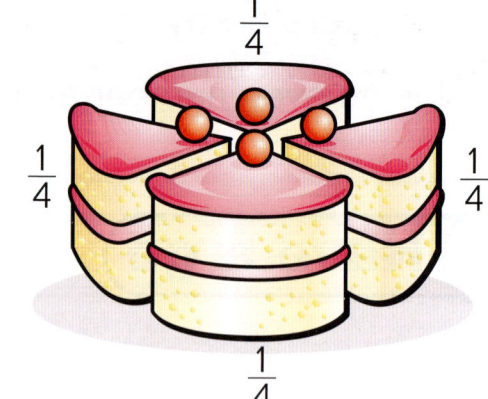

Have a go

1 Colour **one quarter** of each shape.

 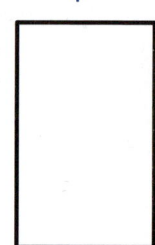    

2 Colour **one quarter** of each set of sweets. Write the answer.

a $\frac{1}{4}$ of 12 = _____

b $\frac{1}{4}$ of 16 = _____

c $\frac{1}{4}$ of 4 = _____

d $\frac{1}{4}$ of 20 = _____

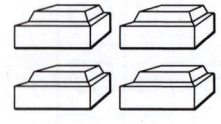

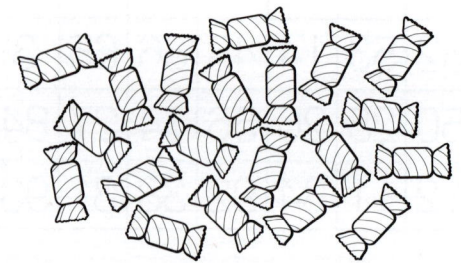

Unit 6: Addition

Remember

You can use a **number track** to help you add. Count on from the biggest number.

What is 4 add 7?

4 + 7 gives the same answer as 7 + 4

Count on 4 from 7: the answer is 11.

Have a go

1 Use the number track to help you work out the missing numbers.

a 4 + ☐ = 9   b ☐ + 4 = 12   c 6 + 7 = ☐

d 6 + ☐ = 11   e ☐ + 7 = 15   f 7 + 9 = ☐

g 3 + ☐ = 10   h ☐ + 8 = 13   i 8 + 6 = ☐

j 7 + ☐ = 12   k ☐ + 5 = 14   l 7 + 7 = ☐

m 5 + ☐ = 13   n ☐ + 6 = 11   o 9 + 6 = ☐

2 Colour the even numbers blue and the odd numbers red.

What number can you see?

2	1	5	17	9	12
8	17	14	8	3	16
16	13	4	10	13	6
4	9	19	7	15	18
12	6	1	19	4	10
16	15	5	3	13	8
18	7	6	8	9	4
6	3	10	12	1	18
12	11	17	5	7	16

Unit 7: Addition problems

Remember

Use **addition facts** to help work out other sums.

4 + 3 = 7   6 + 5 = 11
40 + 30 = 70   60 + 50 = 110

Numbers can be broken up to make adding easier.
35 + 40 is the same as 30 + 40 + 5 = 75

Have a go

1 Write the totals.

a 30 + 60 =   b 50 + 30 =

c 20 + 50 =   d 40 + 40 =

e 60 + 40 =   f 80 + 50 =

g 70 + 60 =   h 90 + 30 =

2 Look at these numbers

30   25   35   50   45

Write two of the numbers in each of these sums to give the totals
shown.

a ☐ + ☐ = 80   b ☐ + ☐ = 55

c ☐ + ☐ = 85   d ☐ + ☐ = 60

e ☐ + ☐ = 75

Unit 8: Subtraction and counting

Remember

If you are finding the **difference** between two numbers, it can be useful to count on using a **number track**.

What is the difference between 11 and 7? $11 - 7 = ?$

Start at 7 and count the jumps to 11. $11 - 7 = 4$

Have a go

1 Show the jumps and write the answers. Remember to count on from the smaller number.

a $12 - 8 =$ ☐

b $15 - 7 =$ ☐

c $16 - 9 =$ ☐

d $18 - 12 =$ ☐

e $17 - 11 =$ ☐

f $19 - 14 =$ ☐

2 Write the differences between these pairs of numbers.

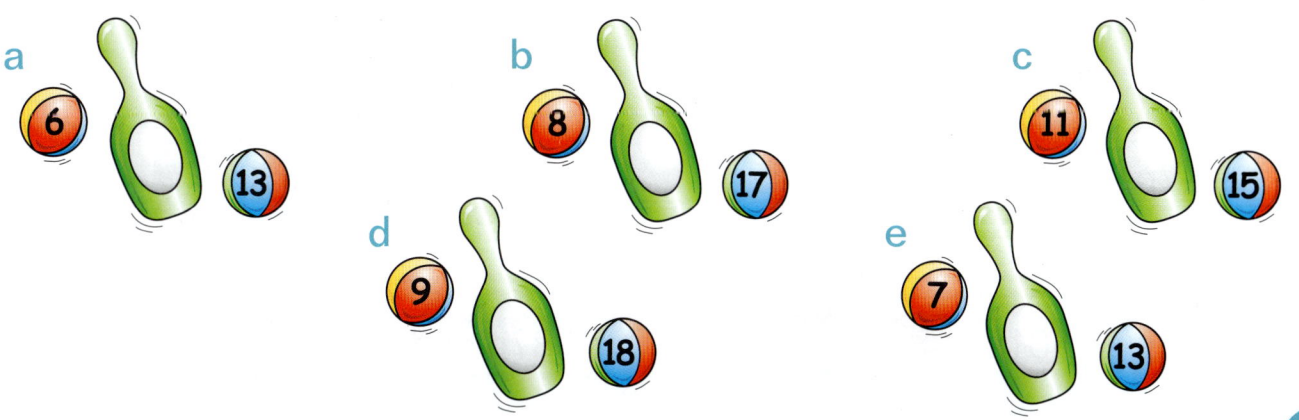

a   b   c

d   e

 Remember

We use these words when we **take away**.

> subtract, difference, less than, fewer

$13 - 8 = 5$

8 fewer than 13 is 5

13 subtract 8 equals 5

8 less than 13 is 5

the difference between 8 and 13 is 5

 Have a go

1 Write the answers.

a The difference between 6 and 10 is [ ]   b 9 less than 12 is [ ]

c 13 subtract 7 equals [ ]   d 6 fewer than 11 is [ ]

e 14 take away 9 equals [ ]   f 17 subtract 9 equals [ ]

g The difference between 8 and 15 is [ ]   h 7 less than 19 is [ ]

2 Write the differences in price between these amounts.

a 38p and 42p  _____   b 29p and 34p  _____

c 47p and 52p  _____   d 68p and 75p  _____

e 56p and 61p _____   f 87p and 93p  _____

Unit 10: Subtraction problems

Remember

Use **subtraction facts** to help you work out other sums.

8 – 5 = 3   12 – 7 = 5
80 – 50 = 30   120 – 70 = 50

Numbers can be broken up to make taking away easier.
80 – 55 is the same as 80 – 50 – 5 = 25
65 – 30 is the same as 60 – 30 + 5 = 35

Have a go

1 Write the answer.

a   70 – 30 =   b   80 – 40 =

c   40 – 20 =   d   90 – 60 =

e   130 – 90 =   f   110 – 50 =

g   140 – 60 =   h   120 – 80 =

2 Look at these numbers.

60   45   25   30   80

Write two of the numbers in each of these subtractions to give
the answers shown.

a   ☐ – ☐ = 50   b   ☐ – ☐ = 15

c   ☐ – ☐ = 20   d   ☐ – ☐ = 35

e   ☐ – ☐ = 55

Unit 11: Money problems

When we give change, we often **count up**.

This ice cream costs 38p.

38p

To work out the change from 50p, count up:
38p ➔ +2p ➔ 40p ➔+10p ➔ 50p   So the change is 12p.

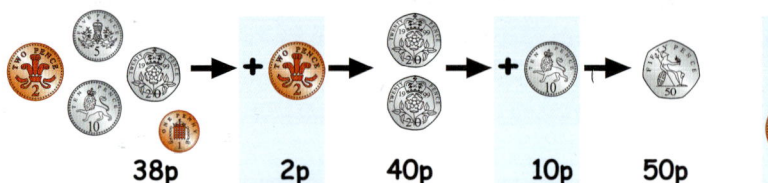

38p   2p   40p   10p   50p   12p

Have a go

① 50p is paid for each of these. Draw the coins you could have as change.

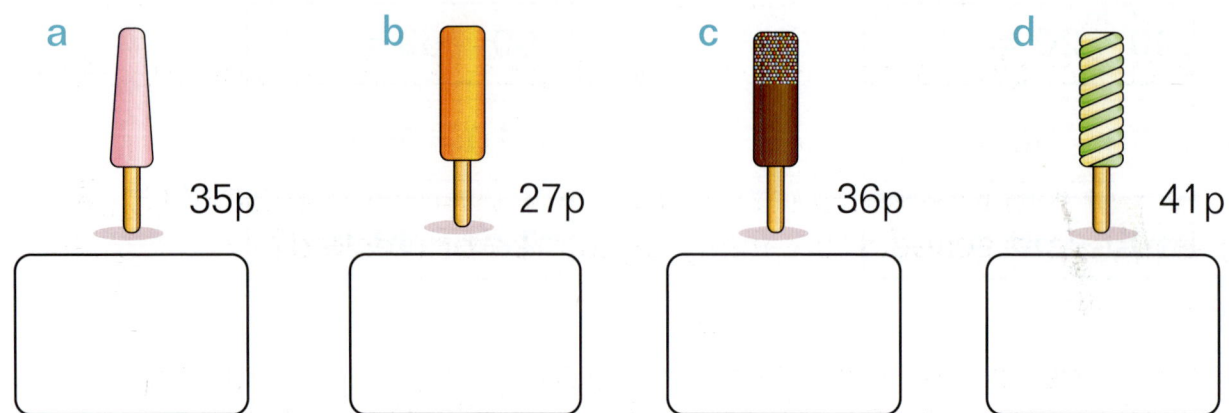

a   35p

b   27p

c   36p

d   41p

② The change given from £1 is shown below. What did each ice cream cost?

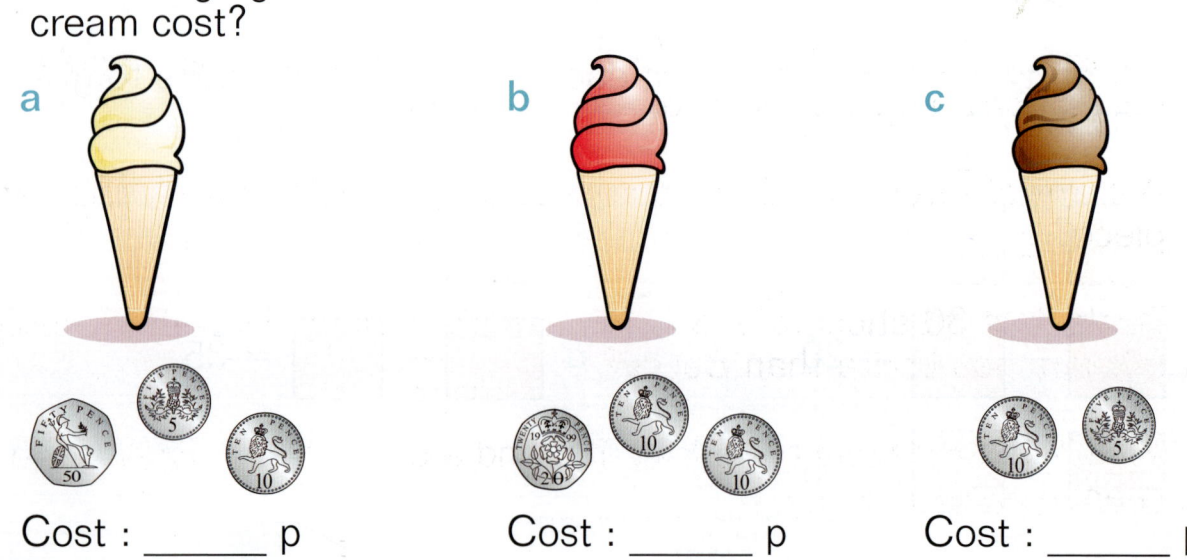

a

b

c

Cost : _____ p   Cost : _____ p   Cost : _____ p

Unit 12: Mixed problems

Remember

Read word problems carefully and look for clues for **adding** or **taking away**.

Adding words
total, sum, altogether, more than, plus, increase

Subtracting words
take away, difference, left, less than, fewer, remain, change, decrease

Answer these word problems.

a   In his swimming lesson, Ben swims 60 metres, rests for a little while, and then swims another 90 metres. How many metres does he swim altogether? _____

b   A pair of gloves costs £4.60. What change will there be from £5? _____

c   Out of two boxes each containing twelve eggs, a total of three eggs are cracked. How many eggs are not cracked?

_____

d   Entrance to a summer fair costs 30p for adults and 10p for children. How much will it cost for a family of two adults and three children? _____

e   A bus has 28 people on it. If four people get on and ten people get off, how many people remain on the bus? _____

f   A piece of ribbon is 28 cm long. If it is cut in half, how long is each piece? _____

g   Becky has 30 stickers and Laura has 55 stickers. How many more stickers has Laura than Becky? _____

h   Ali has £1. He buys a drink at 45p and a cake at 30p. How much change is he given? _____

Unit 13: Multiplying by 5

Remember

This diagram shows:

3 + 3 + 3 + 3 + 3 = 15   5 + 5 + 5 = 15

$3 \times 5 = 15$ $5 \times 3 = 15$

3 multiplied by 5 = 15   5 multiplied by 3 = 15

Have a go

1 Use the pictures to help you answer these.

a $5 \times 6 =$ _____

   $6 \times 5 =$ _____

b $5 \times 4 =$ _____

   $4 \times 5 =$ _____

c $5 \times 7 =$ _____

   $7 \times 5 =$ _____

d $5 \times 5 =$ _____

e $5 \times 9 =$ _____

   $9 \times 5 =$ _____

f $5 \times 8 =$ _____

   $8 \times 5 =$ _____

2 Use a timer. Answer these as quickly as you can.

a $4 \times 5 =$ _____

b $3 \times 2 =$ _____

c $4 \times 2 =$ _____

d $7 \times 5 =$ _____

e $8 \times 2 =$ _____

f $2 \times 5 =$ _____

g $6 \times 2 =$ _____

h $5 \times 5 =$ _____

i $5 \times 2 =$ _____

j $3 \times 5 =$ _____

k $10 \times 2 =$ _____

l $7 \times 2 =$ _____

m $8 \times 5 =$ _____

n $2 \times 2 =$ _____

o $6 \times 5 =$ _____

p $9 \times 5 =$ _____

q $1 \times 5 =$ _____

r $1 \times 2 =$ _____

s $10 \times 5 =$ _____

t $9 \times 2 =$ _____

Try it again. Can you beat your best time?

Remember

Triangles are special **2D shapes**. They have three straight sides.

Have a go

1 Cross out the odd one out in each set. Then complete the sentences describing the remaining shapes.

a This is a set of _____ . They all have _____ sides.

b This is a set of _____ . They all have _____ sides.

c This is a set of _____ . They all have _____ sides.

d This is a set of _____ . They all have _____ sides.

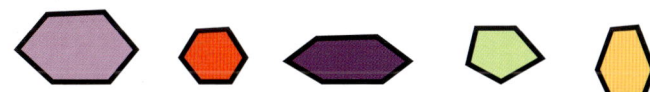

2 Colour all the triangles yellow.
   What have you made?

   _____

A **3D** solid has faces.

A **cube** has six faces.

What is the shape of each face?

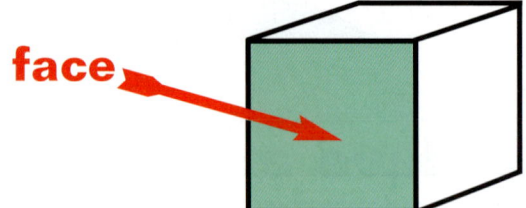

face

1 Join each solid to its faces.

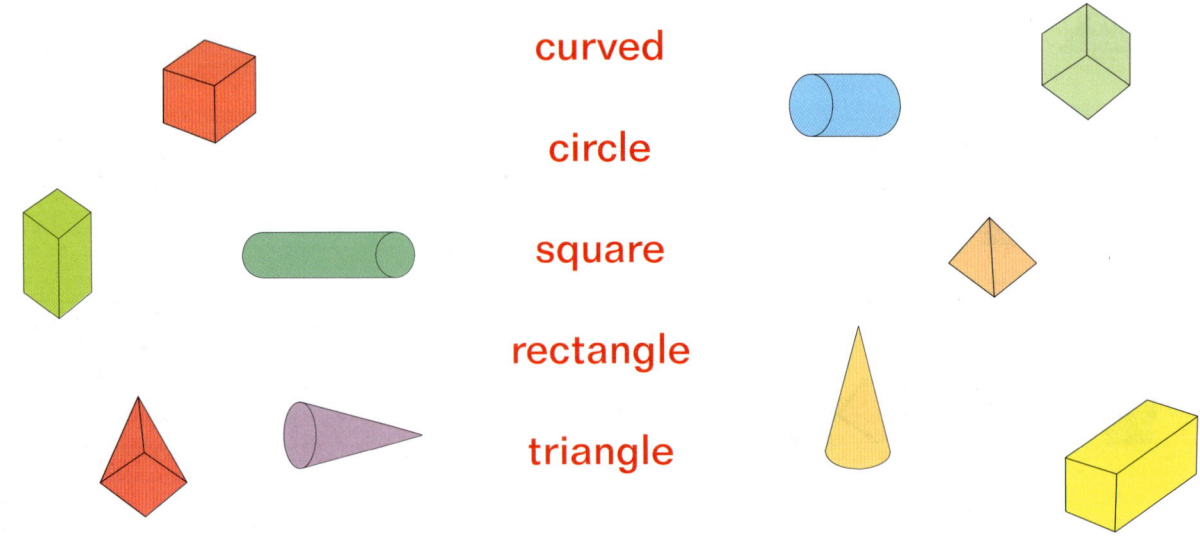

curved

circle

square

rectangle

triangle

2 Name the solids. Write the number of faces for each solid.

a This _____ has ____ square faces and ____ rectangle faces.

b This _____ has ____ circle face and ____ curved face.

c This _____ has ____ circle faces and ____ curved face.

Unit 16: Movement and turning

Remember

We use **left** and **right** to describe which way we turn.
The important thing is that you must turn left and right **from the position you are facing**.

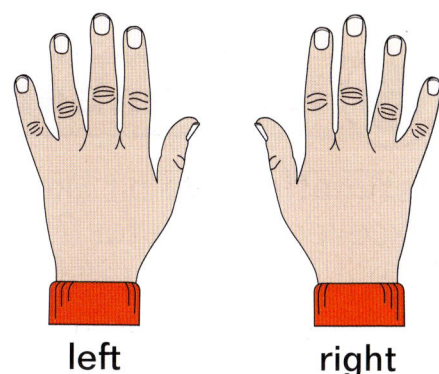

left   right

Have a go

Look at the map. Follow the directions.

Start at A
Forward 1
Turn right
Forward 4
Turn left
Forward 4
Turn left
Forward 13
Where have you finished?

Start at B
Forward 1
Turn right
Forward 2
Turn right
Forward 4
Turn left
Forward 3
Turn right
Forward 1
Where have you finished?

Start at C
Forward 1
Turn right
Forward 1
Turn left
Forward 3
Turn left
Forward 7
Turn right
Forward 8
Turn right
Forward 6
Where have you finished?

Unit 17: Length – estimating

Remember

My estimate is 6 cm.
The exact length is 7 cm.
Quite a close estimate really!

Estimating is a bit like making a good guess. Are you an 'excellent estimator'? This line shows 15 centimetres. Use it to help you estimate lengths.

Have a go

Estimate the length of each of these in centimetres. Then use a ruler to find the exact length.

a Estimate: _____
    Measure: _____

b Estimate: _____
    Measure: _____

c Estimate: _____
    Measure: _____

d Estimate: _____
    Measure: _____

e Estimate: _____
    Measure: _____

f Estimate: _____
    Measure: _____

g Estimate: _____
    Measure: _____

h Estimate: _____
    Measure: _____

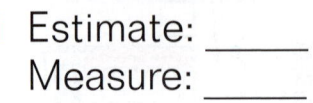

i Estimate: _____
    Measure: _____

j Estimate: _____
    Measure: _____

Unit 18: Measuring capacity

Remember

We find out how much liquid there is in a container by finding its **capacity**.

We use litres (l) and millilitres (ml).

$$1000 \text{ ml} = 1 \text{ litre}$$

Fill a 1 litre jug with water so that you know how much a litre is.

Have a go

⭐ Less than 1 Litre ⭐ Greater than 1 Litre

1. Colour the stars correctly.

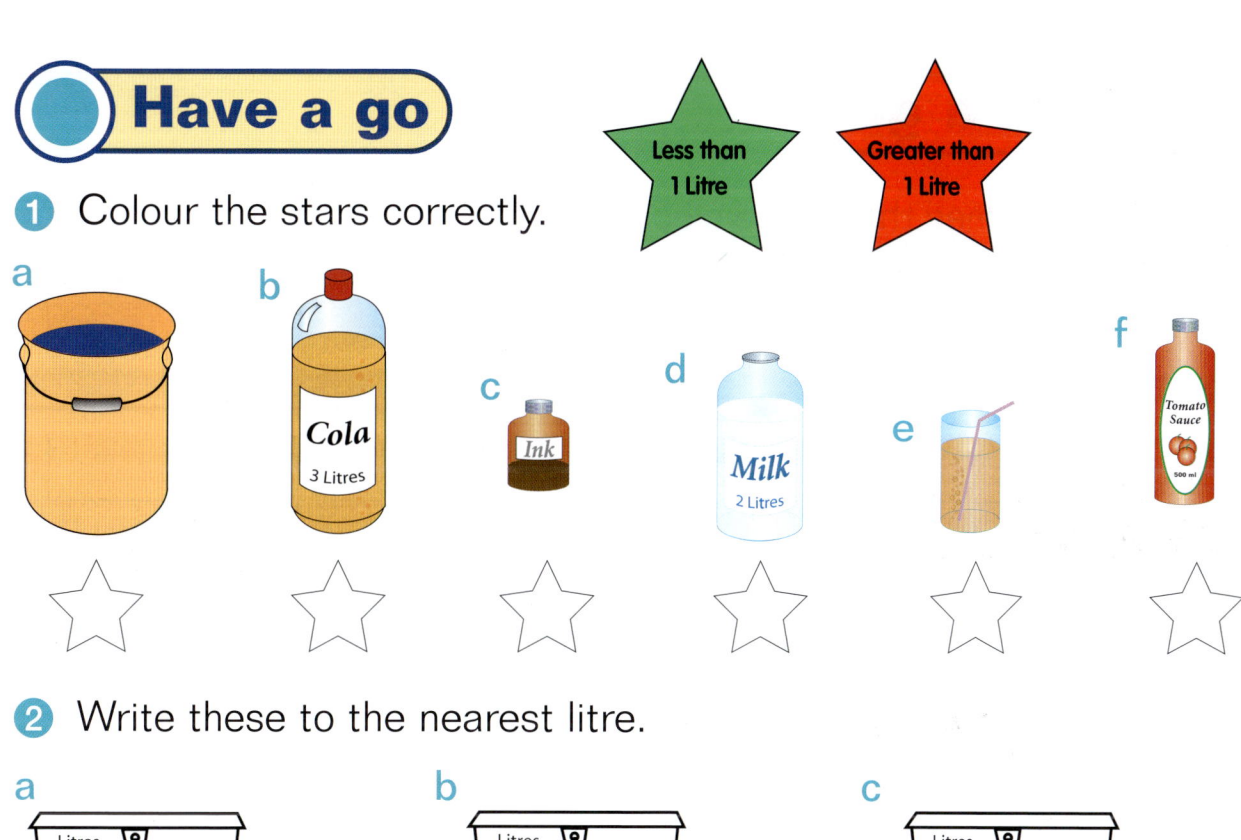

a   b   c   d   e   f

2. Write these to the nearest litre.

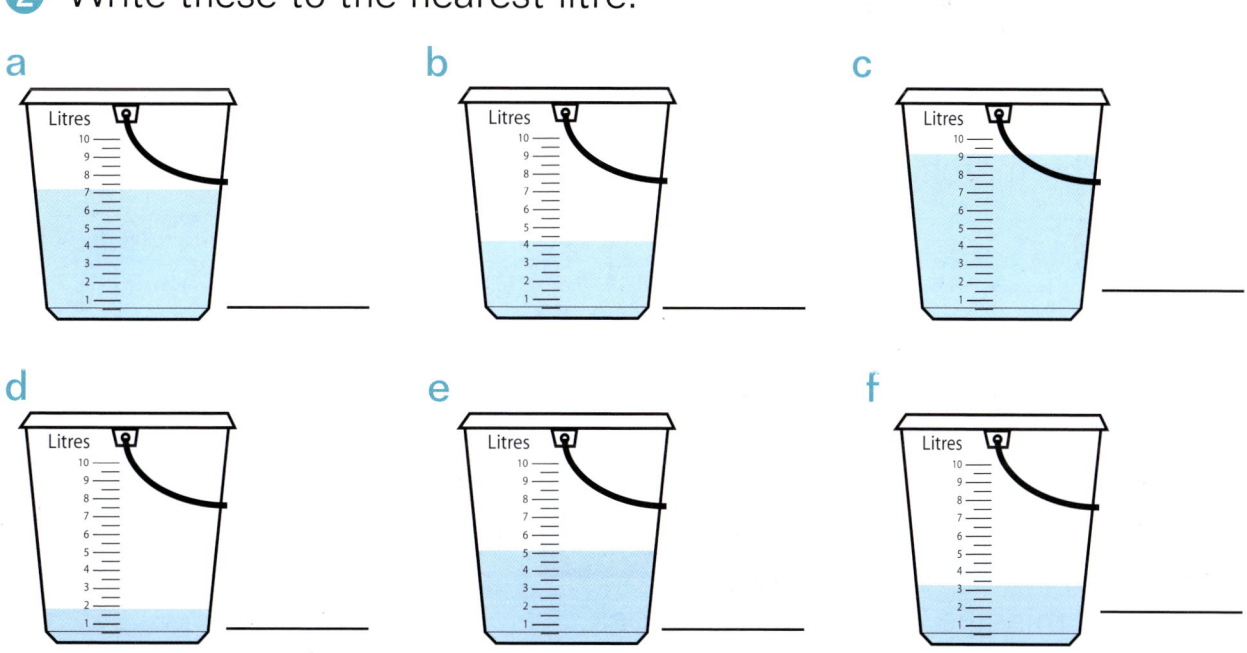

a   b   c

d   e   f

Remember

These two clocks both show 7 o'clock.

These two clocks both show half past 7.

There are **60 minutes in an hour**, so 7:30 is 'half past' the hour. Notice that the hour hand moves halfway towards the next hour.

Have a go

1 Write the times that these clocks show. One has been done for you.

a   4:00   b   [ ]   c   [ ]

d   [ ]   e   [ ]   f   [ ]

g   [ ]   h   [ ]   i   [ ]

j   [ ]

2 Join the matching times on all 3 types of clock.

ten thirty   nine thirty   three thirty   6 o'clock   11 o'clock   four thirty   2 o'clock

2:00   3:30   6:00   9:30   11:00   10:30   4:30

Draw the missing hands on the clock.

Unit 20: Data – pictograms

Remember

Pictograms use **pictures** to show information. Always count the pictures carefully.

Rehanah loves bananas. This shows the number she ate each week for four weeks.

Week 1	🍌 🍌 🍌 🍌 🍌 🍌 🍌
Week 2	🍌 🍌 🍌 🍌 🍌 🍌 🍌 🍌
Week 3	🍌 🍌 🍌 🍌 🍌
Week 4	🍌 🍌 🍌 🍌 🍌 🍌 🍌 🍌

In which week did she eat 8 bananas?

Have a go

1 This shows the results of a survey of the favourite fruits of a group of children.
   Use the pictogram to answer these.

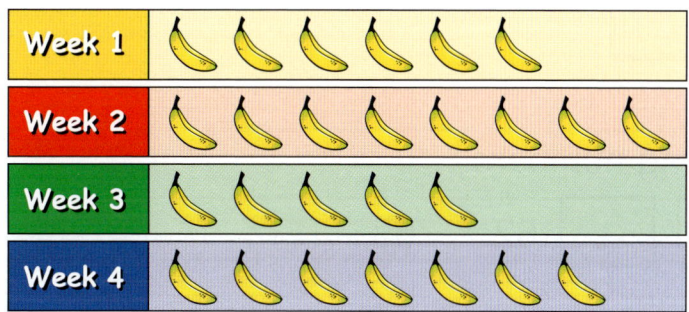

a How many children chose apples?
   _____

b Which fruit was chosen by 3 children?
   _____

c Which was the most popular fruit?
   _____

d Which two fruits were chosen by the same number of children? _____

e How many more children chose grapes than strawberries? _____

f How many children altogether were in the survey? _____

2 Carry out your own survey and draw a pictogram on a blank sheet of paper to show your results.

Test 1

Check how much you have learned.

Answer the questions.
Mark your answers. Fill in your score.

SCORE

1 Write the number.

seventy-four [ ]

out of 1 [ ]

2 Write the missing numbers.

57 [ ] 59 [ ] [ ] 62 63

out of 3 [ ]

3 Estimate the length of this ladder.
Then use a ruler to find the exact length.

Estimate: [ ] cm

Measure: [ ] cm

out of 2 [ ]

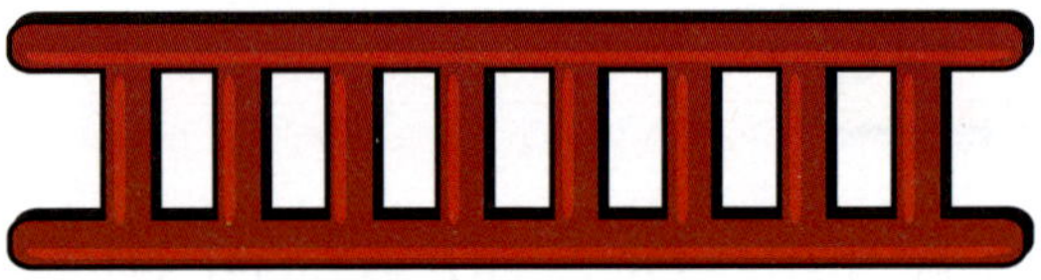

4 This shows the number of goals scored by a football team in five games.

How many more goals were scored in game 1 than in game 5?

____

Game 1
Game 2
Game 3
Game 4
Game 5

out of 1 [ ]

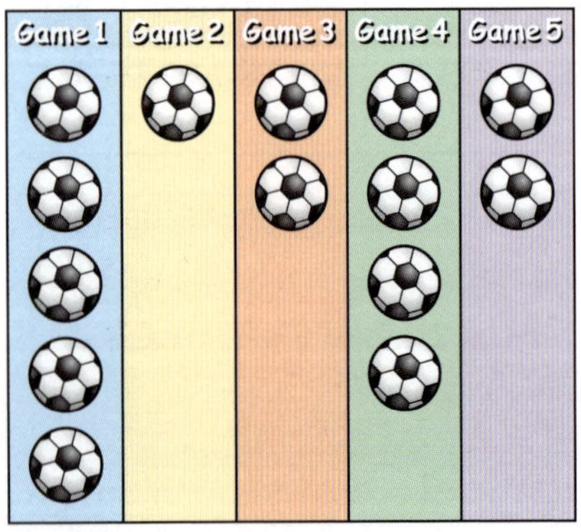

5 Write the missing numbers.

a $7 + \boxed{} = 15$

b $\boxed{} + 4 = 16$

c $9 + 5 = \boxed{}$

6 Answer these.

a $\frac{1}{4}$ of $8 = \boxed{}$

b $\frac{1}{4}$ of $12 = \boxed{}$

7 Tick the triangles in this set of shapes.

8 Write the times that these clocks show.

a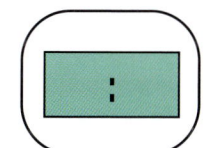

b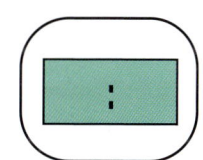

9 What is the difference between these pairs of numbers?

a (9) and (16) ➡

b (12) and (18) ➡

10 What is 19 subtract 11?

25

Test 2

Check how much you have learned.

Answer the questions.
Mark your answers. Fill in your score.

SCORE

1 Circle the even numbers.

46   35   81   78   50   32

out of 1

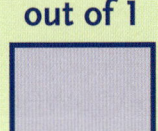

2 How much water to the nearest litre is in this bucket?

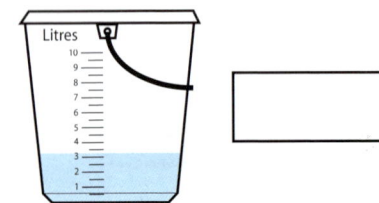

out of 1

3 Write the totals.

a 50 + 60 = _____   b 35 + 40 = _____

out of 2

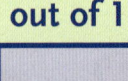

4 Write the answers.

a 120 − 60 = _____   b 85 − 50 = _____

out of 2

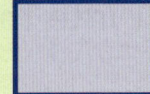

5 Join the matching shapes.

four rectangle faces and
two square faces

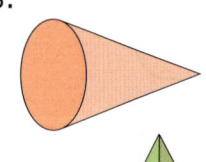 pyramid

one curved face and
one circle face

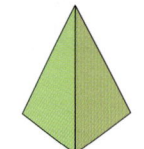 cylinder

one square face and four
triangle faces

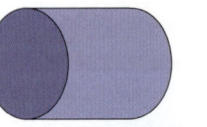 cuboid

one curved face and
two circle faces

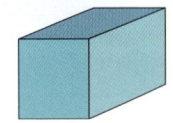 cone

out of 4

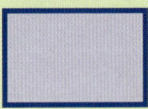

26

6 The car turns left. Which town is it heading for?

_____

7 Circle the largest number in each set.

a  48, 63, 58   b 74, 83, 87

8 Answer these.

a $7 \times 5 =$ ____   b $8 \times 5 =$ ____   c $5 \times 5 =$ ____

9 Write the change from £1 for this magazine.

_____

10 David weighs 45 kg and his brother weighs 30 kg more. How much does his brother weigh?

_____

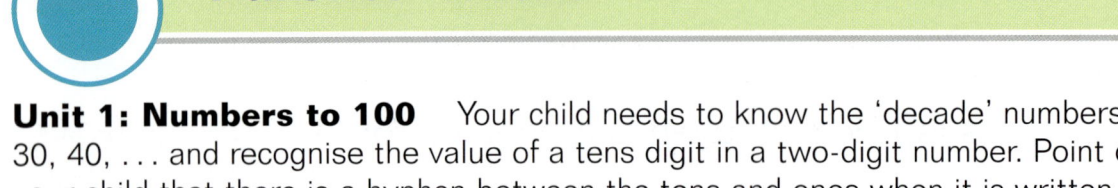

Parents' notes

Unit 1: Numbers to 100   Your child needs to know the 'decade' numbers, 10, 20, 30, 40, . . . and recognise the value of a tens digit in a two-digit number. Point out to your child that there is a hyphen between the tens and ones when it is written as a word – for example, thirty-five.

Unit 2: Comparing numbers   Place value is the position or place of a digit in a number. The same digit has a different value at different places in the number. Encourage your child to see two-digit numbers as tens and ones. So 35 needs to be seen as $30 + 5$. When numbers are compared to see which is larger or smaller, make sure that your child looks at the tens digit of each number and then the ones digit.

Unit 3: Counting on and back   Counting backwards and forwards from different starting-points is an important skill to practise, even as your child gets older. A number line is very useful for learning the order and position of numbers. 'More than' and 'less than' are used to ask about the position of different numbers, which enables the missing numbers in a sequence to be determined.

Unit 4: Odd and even numbers   Your child needs to recognise odd and even numbers up to 100 and beyond. Make sure that your child knows that it is the 'ones' digit that shows whether a number is odd or even. An even number can be divided equally by 2, whereas odd numbers leave a remainder of 1 when divided by 2.

Unit 5: Fractions – quarters   It is important to understand that quartering a shape means making it into four **equal** parts. To find a quarter of an amount or shape your child needs to make four equal parts and look at one of the parts. With questions such as $\frac{1}{4}$ of 12, your child may relate this to dividing by 4 ($12 \div 4$).

Unit 6: Addition   Encourage your child to count on from the given number to the answer in order to work out the missing number. He or she may use the number track to help, or may work it out mentally. These addition facts to 20 should be quickly recalled by your child. Therefore it is a good idea to write down the facts that your child doesn't know, in order to help him or her practise and learn.

Unit 7: Addition problems   Number bonds are pairs of numbers that produce a particular total. It is useful to be able to recall quickly number bonds of all the numbers to 20. Once these are known, they can be used to work out 'decade' additions, such as $50 + 70$. The answer will be ten times bigger than $5+7$, so the relationship between them is easy to see: 120 is ten times more than 12.

Unit 8: Subtraction and counting   There are many different strategies for 'taking away', including counting on and counting back. If you need to find the difference between two numbers, counting on from the smaller number to the larger is a useful strategy. Your child may find it helpful to picture a number track in his or her head.

Unit 9: Subtraction words   The language of maths can be confusing for children, particularly the words involved with subtraction. Use the words in everyday situations and show the link between the words and the use of the subtraction sign.

Unit 10: Subtraction problems   Your child needs to be able to recall quickly subtraction facts, possibly by using the related addition facts. Once these are known, they can be used to work out 'decade' subtractions, such as $140 - 80$. Make sure that your child recognises the pattern, with the answer being ten times bigger than $14 - 8$.

Unit 11: Money problems   Working out how much change to give is done most easily by using the 'shopkeeper's method'. This involves counting on from the cost of the item to the amount given. So, if an item cost 73p and £1 was given, the change would be 2p (up to 75p) + 5p (up to 80p) + 20p (up to £1) → 27p. Practise this by playing 'shops' at home with real coins and shopping items.

Unit 12: Mixed problems   With word problems, encourage your child to read the problem carefully and try to picture the problem as a scene in his or her head. Your child then works out what sort of calculation is needed before answering the problem. Once your child has an answer, he or she needs to look back at the problem to see what exactly it was asking for as an answer and to consider if their answer 'makes sense'.

Unit 13: Multiplying by 5   Grouping fifteen items in fives and counting the groups (5 + 5 + 5) can be written as $3 \times 5 = 15$ (3 lots of 5) or $5 \times 3 = 15$ (5 multiplied by 3). The $\times$ sign is used to mean either 'times' or, more correctly, 'multiplied by'. The important thing for your child to know is that 5×3 and 3×5 give the same answer.

Unit 14: 2D shapes   Each two-dimensional shape with straight sides has a special name related to the number of sides. So, any shape with three straight sides is a triangle. Then, within that set, there are further names for shapes with certain features. Make sure your child recognises that some shapes may have more than one name. For example, a square is a special rectangle and also a type of quadrilateral.

Unit 15: 3D solids   Point out soilds around your house and outside that are shaped like a cube, cuboid, sphere, cone and cylinder. For each solid, ask your child to describe it and point out the faces, describing the shapes of the faces and the number of faces there are.

Unit 16: Movement and turning   Turning left and right on a map or plan is quite difficult because it depends on the direction the person is facing. Practise turning left and right and going forward a number of paces around a course in your house or garden. On the plan make sure that your child always turns left or right from the position he or she is facing. For example, from position C in the map on page 19, he or she is facing towards the next square, across the page.

Unit 17: Length – estimating   Before measuring any length, encourage your child to estimate the approximate length and then measure it to check the accuracy of his or her estimate. Check that he or she can measure accurately with a ruler, using the correct starting point on the ruler.

Unit 18: Measuring capacity   Capacity is measured using litres and millilitres and it is important that your child is able to estimate different amounts such as 100 ml, 500 ml and 1 litre. Look at different sized bottles and containers so that your child can recognise the different amounts.

Unit 19: Time   This unit concentrates on 'o'clock' and 'half past' the hour. Reading the o'clock times usually causes few problems, but it is important to practise these so that when your child reads other times he or she can concentrate on the number of minutes past the hour. Point out that the hour hand moves slowly around towards the next hour as the minute hand goes round.

Unit 20: Data – pictograms   Pictograms are a very popular way of showing information as a graph. Make sure that your child understands that, for these pictograms, each picture represents one item. Your child will also come across pictograms where each picture represents 2, 5 or 10 items. Therefore it is important for your child to read the information about each pictogram so that he or she can interpret it correctly.

Answers

Unit 1: Numbers to 100 (page 4)

1 a 34　b sixty-seven　c 59
　d twenty-eight　e 72
　f ninety-three　g 66
　h forty-five

2 Across
　a 34　b 26　e 61　f 35
　Down
　a 37　c 63　d 52　e 68　g 59

Unit 2: Comparing numbers (page 5)

1 a 39　40　41　42
　b 58　59　60
　c 47　48
　d 62　63　64
　e 78　79　80　81
　f 69　70
　g 86　87　88　89

2 a 76 m　b 48 cm　c 72 kg　d 96p
　e £53　f 97 g　g 67p　h £73
　i 67 kg　j 18 cm

Unit 3: Counting on and back (page 6)

1 a 29　b 40　c 44　d 33　e 39
　f 33　g 48　h 39

2 a 47　51
　b 65　67
　c 71　66
　d 83　82

Unit 4: Odd and even numbers (page 7)

1 a 15　19
　b 22　24
　c 29　25
　d 38　42
　e 32　24
　f 47　45

2 TEN

Unit 5: Fractions – quarters (page 8)

1

2 Check that your child has coloured the correct number of items for each question.
　a 3　b 4　c 1　d 5

Unit 6: Addition (page 9)

1 a 5　b 8　c 13　d 5　e 8　f 16
　g 7　h 5　i 14　j 5　k 9　l 14
　m 8　n 5　o 15

2 8

Unit 7: Addition problems (page 10)

1 a 90　b 80　c 70　d 80　e 100
　f 130　g 130　h 120

2 a 30 + 50 or 35 + 45
　b 30 + 25　c 35 + 50
　d 25 + 35　e 25 + 50 or 30 + 45

Unit 8: Subtraction and counting (page 11)

1 a 4　b 8　c 7　d 6　e 6　f 5

2 a 7　b 9　c 4　d 9　e 6

Unit 9: Subtraction words (page 12)

1 a 4　b 3　c 6　d 5　e 5　f 8
　g 7　h 12

2 a 4p　b 5p　c 5p　d 7p　e 5p　f 6p

Unit 10: Subtraction problems (page 13)

1 a 40　b 40　c 20　d 30　e 40
　f 60　g 80　h 40

2 a 80 − 30　b 45 − 30 or 60 − 45
　c 80 − 60 or 45 − 25
　d 80 − 45 or 60 − 25
　e 80 − 25

Unit 11: Money problems (page 14)

1 Your child may use a variety of coins. Check that they match each amount of change as listed.
  a coins adding to 15p change
  b coins adding to 23p change
  c coins adding to 14p change
  d coins adding to 9p change

2 a 35p b 60p c 85p

Unit 12: Mixed problems (page 15)

a 150 m b 40p c 21 d 90p e 22
f 14 cm g 25 h 25p

Unit 13: Multiplying by 5 (page 16)

1 a 30 b 20 c 35 d 25 e 45 f 40

2 a 20 b 6 c 8 d 35 e 16 f 10
  g 12 h 25 i 10 j 15 k 20 l 14
  m 40 n 4 o 30 p 45 q 5 r 2
  s 50 t 18

Unit 14: 2D shapes (page 17)

1 a triangles   3 sides

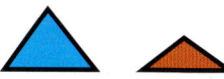 

  b rectangles   4 sides

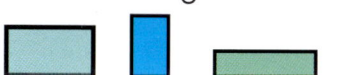

  c pentagons   5 sides

  d hexagons   6 sides

2 A star

Unit 15: 3D solids (page 18)

1

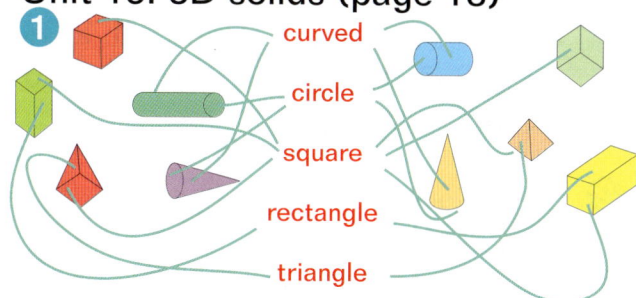

curved
circle
square
rectangle
triangle

2 a This cuboid has 2 square faces and 4 rectangle faces.

  b This cone has 1 circle face and 1 curved face.

  c This cylinder has 2 circle faces and 1 curved face.

Unit 16: Movement and turning (page 19)

Start A → Finish at park
Start B → Finish at fish and chip shop
Start C → Finish at cinema

Unit 17: Length – estimating (page 20)

Check that your child's estimates are close to the real lengths.
a 5 cm b 4 cm c 8 cm d 2 cm
e 2 cm f 6 cm g 4 cm h 3 cm
i 3 cm j 7 cm

Unit 18: Measuring capacity (page 21)

1

2 a 7 litres b 4 litres c 9 litres
  d 2 litres e 5 litres f 3 litres

Unit 19: Time (page 22)

1 a 4:00 b 9:00 c 10:00 d 2:00
e 8:00 f 1:30 g 11:30 h 3:30
i 5:30 j 12:30

2

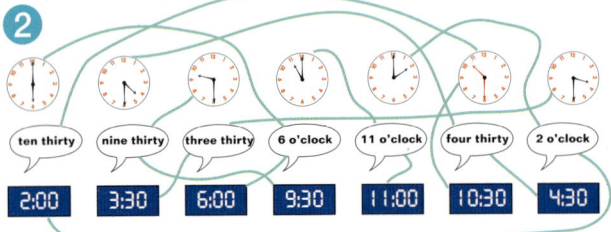

Unit 20: Data – pictograms (page 23)

She ate 8 bananas in week 2.

1 a 6 b oranges c grapes
d bananas and pears e 3 f 30

2 Check that your child's pictogram is accurate.

Test 1 (pages 24 and 25)

1 74

2 58 60 61

3 7 cm

4 3

5 a 8 b 12 c 14

6 a 2 b 3

7 [pentagon] [triangle ✓] [rhombus] [triangle ✓] [pentagon] [hexagon] [triangle ✓]

8 a 11:00 b 2:30

9 a 7 b 6

10 8

Test 2 (pages 26 and 27)

1 46 78 50 32

2 3 litres

3 a 110 b 75

4 a 60 b 35

5

four rectangle faces and two square faces — pyramid

one curved face and one circle face — cylinder

one square face and four triangle faces — cuboid

one curved face and two circle faces — cone

6 Welby

7 a 63 b 87

8 a 35 b 40 c 25

9 15p

10 75 kg